Author:

Kathryn Senior is a former biomedical
research scientist with an advanced degree in
microbiology from Cambridge University, England.
After four years in research, she joined the world
of publishing as an editor of children's science
books. She has now been a full-time science writer
for more than 15 years.

Artist:

Mark Bergin was born in Hastings, England, in
1961. He studied at Eastbourne College of Art and
specializes in historical reconstructions, aviation,
and maritime subjects. He lives in Bexhill-on-Sea,
England, with his wife and children.

Series creator:

David Salariya was born in Dundee, Scotland.
He has illustrated a wide range of books and has
created and designed many new series for
publishers in the UK and overseas. David
established The Salariya Book Company in 1989.
He lives in Brighton, England, with his wife,
illustrator Shirley Willis, and their son, Jonathan.

Editor: **Stephen Haynes**

Editorial Assistant: **Mark Williams**

Published in Great Britain in 2010 by
The Salariya Book Company Ltd
25 Marlborough Place, Brighton BN1 1UB

ISBN-13: 978-0-531-20506-8 (lib. bdg.)   978-0-531-13786-4 (pbk.)
ISBN-10: 0-531-20506-1 (lib. bdg.)   0-531-13786-4 (pbk.)

All rights reserved.
Published in 2010 in the United States
by Franklin Watts
An imprint of Scholastic Inc.
Published simultaneously in Canada.

A CIP catalog record for this book is available
from the Library of Congress.

Printed and bound in China.
Printed on paper from sustainable sources.
1 2 3 4 5 6 7 8 9 10 R 19 18 17 16 15 14 13 12 11 10

PAPER FROM
SUSTAINABLE
FORESTS

You Wouldn't Want to Be a Nurse During the American Civil War!

Written by
Kathryn Senior

Illustrated by
Mark Bergin

Created and designed by
David Salariya

A Job That's Not for the Squeamish

Franklin Watts®
An Imprint of Scholastic Inc.
NEW YORK • TORONTO • LONDON • AUCKLAND • SYDNEY
MEXICO CITY • NEW DELHI • HONG KONG
DANBURY, CONNECTICUT

Contents

Introduction

It's May 1861 and you're going on the adventure of your life! You work for a newspaper in New York City and want to be a famous reporter. When your editor asks you to cover the fighting that began last month, you jump at the chance.

No one knows how long this conflict will last. It started when southern states withdrew from the United States and formed a new nation, the Confederate States of America. Many Southerners worried that the new U.S. president, Abraham Lincoln, would outlaw slavery.

Northerners are divided about whether slavery should be outlawed. But most back President Lincoln, who promises to force the southern states back into the United States. Americans have now started fighting and killing each other. This could be the start of a full-scale civil war!

This is like nothing we've ever seen before!

You're excited by the job, but you're worried too. What if you get shot? How will you cope with seeing men killed and injured in battle?

■ Union (northern) states

☐ Confederate (southern) states

■ Border states

☐ Western territories

CANADA

MEXICO

It's a Bloodbath!

The war has been going on for a year now. The fighting is lasting much longer than anyone expected. The battles are huge. At the Battle of Shiloh in April 1862, over 60,000 soldiers from the Union fight about 40,000 Confederate soldiers. By the end of the battle, 23,746 men are dead or wounded and 3,000 horses are dead. The scene after a battle is a terrible sight, with broken bodies everywhere.

You don't know it yet, but the American Civil War will last four years, until 1865. The most soldiers killed or wounded in a single battle will be 51,112, at the Battle of Gettysburg, which takes place over three days, July 1–3, 1863. Altogether, about 620,000 soldiers will be killed during the Civil War.

THE NAPOLEON 12-pound smoothbore cannon is widely used by both sides in the Civil War. Larger guns called howitzers fire powerful explosive shells. These large guns are very deadly, particularly when fired at close range.

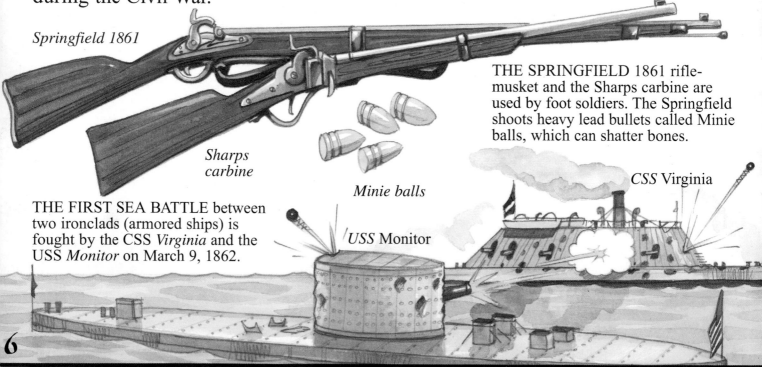

Springfield 1861

Sharps carbine

Minie balls

THE SPRINGFIELD 1861 rifle-musket and the Sharps carbine are used by foot soldiers. The Springfield shoots heavy lead bullets called Minie balls, which can shatter bones.

CSS Virginia

USS Monitor

THE FIRST SEA BATTLE between two ironclads (armored ships) is fought by the CSS *Virginia* and the USS *Monitor* on March 9, 1862.

ARMORED TRAINS are used during the Civil War for the first time anywhere in the world. This one runs on the railroad between Baltimore and Havre de Grace, Maryland.

Handy Hint

Take cover! Even though you're a civilian, you could still be caught in the crossfire.

Something's got to be done about this...

At the start of the Civil War, there are few nurses or ambulances. The injured have to help each other off the battlefield.

Disease: The Hidden Enemy

When the war breaks out in 1861, there's very little medical technology. Hardly anyone knows about microscopes or stethoscopes. All doctors are called "surgeons" during this time, but of the 14,000 surgeons who will take part in the war, few have ever done an operation. They have no idea about germs or bacteria. They use the same dirty hands to examine and treat different patients. This spreads diseases and infections. More soldiers will die of dysentery (severe diarrhea) than from battle wounds. Many soldiers will survive being wounded only to die later from infections.

AT LEAST a million soldiers in the Civil War are under 18. John Clem joins the Michigan Volunteer Infantry at age 12. He is wounded twice but lives to become the youngest noncommissioned officer in U.S. Army history—at 13!

Hardened Fighting Men? Hardly!

MOST SOLDIERS are ordinary farm boys— America is still very rural in the 1860s. But there are some soldiers with professional training. Doctors who join up to fight end up becoming army doctors to care for the wounded.

MANY SOLDIERS on both sides can't read or write. One in three soldiers in the Civil War finds it difficult to make sense of written orders.

Nursing in the 1860s

Nursing didn't exist as a profession in America before the Civil War. There were no nurses and few real hospitals. That's all changing during the Civil War, thanks to the 2,000 women who serve as battlefield nurses for both sides.

Male doctors in the 19th century don't want female nurses and try to stop them from "interfering." But soldiers appreciate the help and care that the nurses give them. This encourages women to fight to take care of wounded soldiers. Clara Barton, Dorothea Dix, Harriet Tubman, and others will go down in history for their heroism during the Civil War.

Linda Richards will be the first American nurse to become fully trained, but not until 1873—eight years after the end of the war.

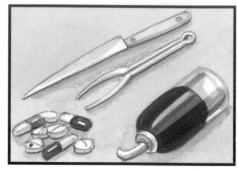

IN THE 1860s, blood transfusions are not yet possible, there are no sterile instruments, and antibiotics won't be available for another 80 years!

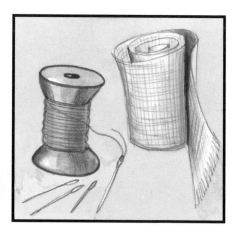

SUTURES AND BANDAGES are sometimes available, but not always (see Handy Hint).

CHLOROFORM can be used to put patients to sleep while a limb is amputated (see page 19).

NOT ENOUGH NURSES. Even though many women volunteer to be nurses in hospitals and on the battlefield, there are too few to go around. After a battle, they have to work around the clock. Many keep going even when they get sick themselves.

If it's any comfort, young man, I don't feel much better than you do.

Handy Hint

Think on your feet! Nurses with no bandages use corn husks and leaves to cover soldiers' wounds.

Local Women Help Out

Many small towns, farms, and homesteads are caught up in the Civil War. Tillie Pierce, who lives in Gettysburg, Pennsylvania, is only 15 when her village becomes the center of one of the biggest battles of the Civil War. She sees things that would terrify an adult, watching as surgeons amputate the badly injured or infected arms and legs of wounded soldiers. Instead of running away, she helps by tearing muslin into bandages for the surgeons to use.

TILLIE PIERCE is at school when a Confederate army storms Gettysburg, closely followed by a mass of Union infantry. Tillie is taken to a neighbor's house, away from the fiercest fighting. For the next week, she does what she can to help the wounded soldiers who arrive at her neighbor's house.

Every Little Bit Helps

EVEN THOSE with no medical skills find many useful ways to help the wounded.

Sorry if it's a bit lumpy.

Mmmfw

TILLIE and other women prepare bandages and compresses to dress the soldiers' wounds.

THEY COOK FOOD and spoon-feed patients who are too exhausted and weak to help themselves.

SOME BRAVE WOMEN search for wounded soldiers who have been left for dead on the battlefield.

LOCAL WOMEN write letters to the young soldiers' families to let them know that their boys are safe.

ONE IMPORTANT JOB is to keep the soldiers feeling positive once the worst of the battle is over.

WASHING AND CLEANING is not a glamorous job, but it certainly helps to make the patients more comfortable.

The World of a Civil War Nurse

DOROTHEA DIX (left) persuades women to volunteer as army nurses. Before the war, she had worked to improve government care for the mentally ill.

Many brave volunteer nurses risk their lives to rescue wounded soldiers from the battlefield. Some of them keep diaries, and after the war they will write about their experiences.

Some nurses, like Tillie Pierce, look after soldiers when the fighting comes to their town. Others, like Clara Barton, volunteer to help wherever they are needed. Barton starts by organizing medical supplies for battle-stricken areas. In 1862, the Surgeon General gives her permission to take ambulances, supplies, and nurses to care for the sick and wounded.

SALLY TOMPKINS (right) sets up a hospital in Richmond, Virginia. She insists on cleanliness, and her hospital saves far more lives than any other. She is made a captain in the Confederate Army.

SUSIE KING TAYLOR (below) is only 12 when the Civil War breaks out. Married at 13, she nurses the soldiers in her husband's regiment.

MARY ANN BICKERDYKE (right) searches battlefields to find wounded soldiers. She also fights for cleaner conditions in hospitals.

HARRIET TUBMAN (above), originally a slave from Maryland, becomes both a nurse and a spy for the Union Army in South Carolina.

14

AT THE BATTLE OF ANTIETAM in September 1862, Clara Barton feels her sleeve "flutter." Looking down, she finds that the soldier she was helping is dead. A bullet has passed through her sleeve and into his chest.

Handy Hint

Wear ear plugs! Otherwise the noise of battle could permanently damage your hearing.

"I have never mended that hole in my sleeve."
—*Clara Barton*

ANNIE ETHERIDGE is a nurse but she joins the Union Army and rides into battle. She nurses the wounded and gives sips of water to the dying.

At the Field Hospital

The first stop for a wounded soldier is a field hospital near the battlefield. This is a hastily built group of tents. Most field hospitals are overcrowded and filthy. There is not much that doctors can do to treat the wounded. Those who are shot in the chest or stomach usually die. Wounded arms and legs are cut off. A doctor can amputate a leg in ten minutes and then move on to the next patient. The nurses take care of the soldiers and bandage their wounds. Still, many patients die of infection.

1. TUESDAY: Many wounded were brought in after today's battle. A lot of soldiers died—we just couldn't save them.

You'll just have to bite the bullet,* son.

2. WEDNESDAY: Ran out of chloroform again, so all amputations have to be done without anesthetic! The screams are terrible—I don't know how I can bear it.

Day by Day

THIS NURSE'S DIARY is based on a real-life account:

4. FRIDAY: One of the soldiers we managed to save was reunited with his wife. She's a nurse at the field hospital!

3. THURSDAY: Amputations save lives, but the loss of an arm or leg is a terrible blow.

**This means "face up to something bad."
But it's said that soldiers really did bite bullets to help them endure pain.*

16

Surgery in the Field

Wounded soldiers are brought off the battlefield in a terrible state. Minie balls and other ammunition shatter bones and tear through flesh.

When a soldier has a badly damaged arm or leg, surgeons have no choice but to cut off the injured limb and hope for the best. Chloroform is used as an anesthetic before the limb is amputated. It is dripped into a cone over the soldier's face until he is unconscious. The surgeon then gets to work quickly, before the patient wakes up again.

Chloroform, discovered in 1831, is used on 800,000 patients during the Civil War.

CHLOROFORM is dangerous! A sealed bottle of the stuff can explode if it's exposed to high heat. Keep the matches far away!

Tools of the Trade

A BONE SAW, a bullet extractor, sharp knives, and scissors for cutting bone are all part of a surgeon's amputation kit. Forceps are also used to clamp the main artery to prevent too much bleeding.

AFTER THE WAR, soldiers with amputated limbs have a hard time finding work. Many have to beg for food and money.

SOME SURGEONS have soldiers lined up ready for limbs to be cut off. The surgeon holds the saw or knife in his teeth so his hands are free to lift the next patient onto the table. A few drops of chloroform, two quick swipes of the knife on his apron, and after a few strokes of the saw, an arm or leg is on the floor.

Nurse administering chloroform

A Convalescent Hospital

Soldiers who survive the horrors of a field hospital are transferred to a convalescent hospital—a hospital for recovering patients—farther away from the battle lines. At the start of the Civil War, there were only a few military hospitals. With no time to build new ones, other buildings are taken over and used as hospitals. Some soldiers are sent to the Patent Office in Washington, D.C., which is hastily converted into a large army hospital.

There are nurses in these hospitals, but the conditions are still bad. Many patients won't live to see the end of the war. One hospital in Virginia is given the official name "Camp Convalescent," but the soldiers call it "Camp Misery." It's an awful place. Soldiers who are completely disabled by their wounds are kept there until they can go home or be exchanged as prisoners of war.

FAMOUS POET Walt Whitman goes to hospitals near Washington, D.C., to search for his brother George, who was wounded in 1862. Whitman sees the full horror of the war and volunteers to become an army nurse.

AT FIRST, there is no proper ambulance service. Many patients die while being carried to hospitals in bumpy wagons.

In 1864, the Rucker ambulance is approved. Long lines of these ambulances pick up the wounded and take them to hospitals.

CLARA BARTON tells a badly wounded soldier that he has only a few minutes to live. "He did not show any fear. They never do."

Nursing on Ships

MOTHER ANGELA GILLESPIE founds the Holy Cross Nursing Sisters, who work in the Mississippi area during the Civil War. Mother Angela also nurses at hospitals in Kentucky, Illinois, Tennessee, and Washington, D.C.

Hospital ships play an important role in the Civil War. One of the most famous is the *Red Rover*, a Confederate steamer that is captured by Union forces and turned into a U.S. Army hospital ship in June 1862. After the Battle of St. Charles in Arkansas, it carries badly burned men up the Mississippi to hospitals in Illinois. Later the *Red Rover* becomes a U.S. Navy hospital ship, staffed by Sisters of the Order of the Holy Cross. Mother Angela Gillespie (left) is one of them.

During its time in service, the *Red Rover* treats about 2,500 wounded men and delivers medical supplies to areas where they are most needed.

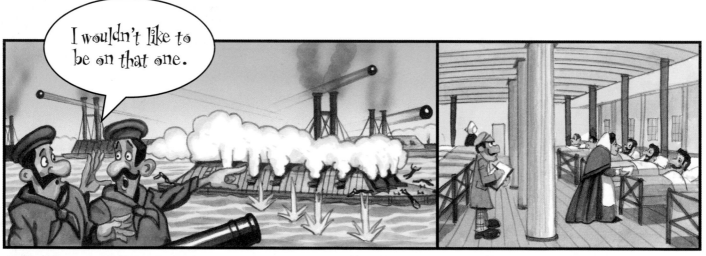

ONE OF the *Red Rover*'s first jobs is to help survivors of the Battle of St. Charles in Arkansas on June 17, 1862. During this battle, the boiler of the Union ironclad *Mound City* is hit by enemy gunfire. Steam from the exploding boiler kills more than two thirds of the crew, and most of the survivors are badly burned.

THE *RED ROVER* is very well equipped. It has its own operating theater, wards for patients, and proper kitchens to prepare good food for them.

Handy Hint

Don't get seasick! The water gets choppy during a battle—even on a river.

U.S.N. HOSPITAL

The nurses on the Red Rover *are* pioneers. They lead the way for the U.S. Navy Nurse Corps, established in 1908.

Take him on board and we'll do what we can.

Lying and Spying

All Civil War nurses are brave, but some show exceptional courage. They lead a double life—either by spying or by disguising themselves as men so they can fight as well as nurse.

Sarah Emma Edmonds fights for the Union disguised as Private Frank Thompson. She spies on the enemy, nurses the wounded, and carries mail.

Mary Edwards Walker was one of the first women in the U.S. to graduate from medical school, in 1855. The army will not allow her to be a surgeon, so she serves as a nurse. Eventually she becomes the first female U.S. Army surgeon in September 1863.

LONG, WIDE SKIRTS with petticoats (right) are in fashion in the 1860s, and it's easy to hide weapons and supplies underneath! Soldiers on guard rarely suspect a thing.

KADY BROWNELL (below) carries the U.S. flag into the first battle of the Civil War in July 1861. In January 1862 she carries the flag again, but she also nurses the wounded.

Howdy, ma'am!

Rustle

CLANK!

Frank *Sarah*

Handy Hint

Pretend to be a washerwoman. The enemy won't pay you any attention while you listen to their secret plans.

Will you fight for freedom?

SARAH EMMA EDMONDS joins the 2nd Michigan Infantry by pretending to be Franklin Flint Thompson. After serving as a male field nurse, she takes part in the battles of Bull Run, Antietam, and Fredericksburg. Then she is sent on dangerous missions to spy behind enemy lines. The army doesn't find out that she is a woman until she writes her memoir after the war.

HARRIET TUBMAN is an escaped slave who works as a nurse and a spy. She leads an armed raid on the Combahee River and frees more than 700 slaves. She persuades many more to leave their enslavers and join the Union Army. She hopes that if the Union states win the war, slavery will be abolished. (And she turns out to be right.)

Finding the Missing

ANDERSONVILLE, a Confederate camp in Georgia, is the most notorious prison camp, but Union camps are rough as well. Many soldiers starve to death while being held as prisoners of war.

After the war, Civil War nurses do not forget the soldiers they had cared for. Clara Barton sets up a program to help find missing soldiers. She goes to Camp Parole in Maryland and interviews people returning from prisoner-of-war camps in the South. She asks them for information about soldiers who may have been left behind. Barton is able to find some men and help reunite them with their families.

Prisoners taken by both sides are not treated well during the war. Many end up in prison camps where conditions are terrible and death from starvation and disease is common.

DORENCE ATWATER, a prisoner of war at Andersonville, smuggles out a list of all the men who he knew had died at the camp. After the war, President Lincoln sends him back to Andersonville with Clara Barton and a team of woodworkers. Atwater's careful list allows the team to identify 13,000 of the dead and mark their graves with their names. Without Atwater, these men would have no memorial.

In 1878, the wooden grave markers are replaced with stone markers.

Such a waste!

AFTER THE WAR is over, people beg Clara Barton for information about missing soldiers. She manages to help reunite some families. But in most cases, the news is not good. Still, knowing where a husband, father, or son died, and marking the place with a grave, is important for many families.

Handy Hint

Mark your graves carefully. Future generations may want to trace their roots.

My, you kids have grown!

We thought we'd never see you again!

A Better Future

While the brave nurses of the American Civil War were taking care of the wounded, a businessman from Switzerland was helping to create an international organization that would provide care for wounded soldiers from all countries. Henry Dunant had been shocked by the aftermath of a battle in Solferino, Italy, in 1859. Thousands of soldiers lay wounded on the battlefield, and no one was helping them. Dunant organized locals to build temporary hospitals and nurse the wounded from both sides. In 1862, he wrote a book calling for the protection of the wounded and the neutral medical workers who nursed them. In 1863, at a meeting in Geneva, Switzerland, Dunant's ideas led to the creation of the International Red Cross.

AFTER THE CIVIL WAR is over, Clara Barton travels to Europe and meets people involved in the Red Cross. This inspires her to found the American Red Cross in 1881.

HENRY DUNANT arrives at Solferino on the day of the battle in 1859. He is horrified to see 38,000 wounded, dying, or dead men, just left behind on the battlefield.

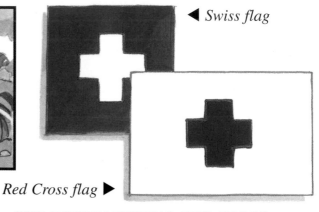

◀ *Swiss flag*

Red Cross flag ▶

THE INTERNATIONAL RED CROSS, which is active in more than 60 countries, is based in Switzerland. The Red Cross flag is modeled on the Swiss national flag.

TODAY, IN ADDITION to helping victims of war, the American Red Cross provides relief to people all over the world who have been affected by disasters.

Because the cross is a Christian symbol, the Red Crescent symbol is used in Islamic countries.

Handy Hint

Stay up to date! Look online for more information about the Red Cross and its work.

What would we do without you people?

MEMBERS of the International Red Cross and Red Crescent rush to the scene of thousands of disasters every year. Members and volunteers provide water, medicine, supplies, and comfort to people who desperately need help.

Glossary

Ammunition Anything fired from a gun or cannon, such as bullets, Minie balls, and cannonballs.

Amputation Surgery to cut off a limb that has been badly damaged and cannot be saved.

Anesthetic A drug that makes patients unconscious so that they don't feel pain during an operation.

Antibiotics Drugs that started to be used in the 1940s to treat infections caused by bacteria.

Armored train A train covered in metal armor to protect it against enemy fire.

Artillery Heavy guns or cannons, usually on wheels.

Bacteria Tiny, single-celled organisms. Some types of bacteria can cause infection and disease.

Blood transfusion A modern medical treatment to replace blood loss from an injury or surgery.

Border states During the Civil War, the five states that permitted slavery yet remained loyal to the United States.

Carbine A short, lightweight rifle.

Chloroform The most commonly used anesthetic during the Civil War.

Civilian A person who is not a member of the armed forces.

Civil war A war between rival groups of people who live in the same country.

Compress A pad of material pressed to a wound to stop bleeding.

Confederate States of America The nation formed by the southern states that broke away from the United States in 1861.

Convalescent hospital A hospital away from the battlefield where soldiers were taken to recover from their wounds.

Dysentery A disease that causes very bad diarrhea. It can cause a person to die from too much water loss.

Field hospital A temporary hospital set up near the battlefield so the wounded can receive immediate treatment.

Forceps A metal clamp that attaches to a blood vessel to prevent bleeding.

Infantry Soldiers who fight on foot.

Infection An invasion of the body by harmful bacteria or other tiny organisms. Infections are more common in crowded, dirty conditions.

Ironclad A steam-powered warship covered in metal armor.

Microscope An instrument with magnifying lenses, used to look at things that are too small to be seen with the naked eye.

Musket A long gun that's loaded through the end of its barrel.

Muslin A thin cotton material often used to make sheets.

Neutral Not taking sides in a conflict.

Noncommissioned officer A soldier who has been promoted from the ranks to be a corporal or a sergeant.

Slave A person who has no freedom and is forced to work without pay for his or her enslaver.

Slavery The practice of owning people as if they were property. Slavery was banned in the United States at the end of the Civil War in 1865.

Sterile Heated or cleaned to be free of harmful bacteria.

Stethoscope A device used by doctors to listen to a patient's heart and lungs.

Suture A stitch used by a surgeon to close a wound.

Territory A region that is controlled by the United States but has not been admitted as a state.

Union During the Civil War, the states that remained loyal to the national government of the United States.

Index